BONUS

Want a Bonus?

Download The Vision Board Freebie:
5 Steps to Create a Vision Board that Works E-Book
&
Vision Board Goal Setting Workbook
Link: bit.ly/vision_board_freebie

60 Positive Affirmation cards · 30 Inspirational quote cards For Vision Boards

I AM CAPABLE AND I AM STRONG.

YOU LEARN MORE FROM FAILURE THAN SUCCESS. DON'T LET IT STOP YOU. FAILURE BUILDS CHARACTER

IF I WANT SOMETHING BADLY ENOUGH, I CAN FIND A WAY TO MAKE IT HAPPEN.

I AM BRAVE, RESILIENT AND STRONG.

THE FUTURE MAY BE UNCERTAIN BUT THAT WON'T STOP ME LOOKING FORWARD WITH HOPE.

ONLY SURROUND YOURSELF WITH PEOPLE WHO WILL LIFT YOU HIGHER

60 Positive Affirmation cards + 30 Inspirational quote cards For Your Vision Board

⬇ DOWNLOAD

Link: bit.ly/affirmations-quotes-cards

Or Use QR Code

FOLLOW US

Follow Us On Instagram: @manifesthappinesschannel
Subscribe to Our Youtube Channel:
youtube.com/c/manifesthappinesschannel

Instagram QR Code

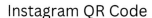

MANIFESTHAPPINESSCHANNEL

For More Vision Board Clip Art Books
Visit Our Page on AMAZON

Link: bit.ly/mh_press

or Use QR Code

We Have Vision Board Clip Art Books For :

Women, Men, Teens, Kids, Travel, Self-love, Weight Loss, Wedding, Word Art, Health, Affirmations, Vision Board Parties, Business & Money and more

FRiENDS

friendship

friends

bestie

Family

Family comes first

HOME

I ♥ My Family

PROM 2007

PROM SEASON IS HERE

PROM

Prom Queen

Congrats
Graduate
IT
ALWAYS
SEEMS
IMPOSSIBLE
UNTIL
it is
DONE

Graduate

HARVARD

OXFORD

STANFORD

ACCEPTED
INTO
UNIVERSITY

BIRTHDAY PARTY

Birthday
GIRL

Influencer

Followers

1k likes

Fitness

Gym

Drink Water

SLEEP WELL

Strong Immunity

Eat Healthy

boost your immune system

TRAVEL THE WORLD

Beach

Vacation

BEAUTY

SLOW DOWN

PRACTICE
YOGA

YOGA

mindfulness

Meditation

MONEY

☆ BANK OF THE UNIVERSE   DATE _____   888

111 Prosperity Road
Milky Way

PAY TO THE ORDER OF _____ $ _____

_____ DOLLARS

MEMO _____   *The Universe*

AUTHORIZED SIGNATURE

111 222 777 111 000 888

☆ BANK OF THE UNIVERSE   DATE _____   888

111 Prosperity Road
Milky Way

PAY TO THE ORDER OF _____ $ _____

_____ DOLLARS

MEMO _____   *The Universe*

AUTHORIZED SIGNATURE

111 222 777 111 000 888

SUCCESS

SUCCESS

Sucessful

Entrepreneur

Online Bussiness

ONLINE BUSINESS

ENTREPRENEUR

BUSINESS PLAN

I Deserve Love and Happiness

I am Enough

I am Worthy

I am Happy

I am Brave

I am Bold

I am Smart

I am Kind

I am Loved

I am Worthy of Everything I Want

Made in the USA
Las Vegas, NV
05 January 2024

83947941R00024